BARBARA ADAMS

PREDYNASTIC EGYPT

D1015360

SHIRE EGYPTOLOGY

2

Cover illustration
White cross-lined, red polished pottery bowl from Mahasna
with modelled hippopotami around the rim, Amratian (Manch. 5069).
(Reproduced by permission of the Manchester Museum.)

British Library Cataloguing in Publication Data available

Published by
SHIRE PUBLICATIONS LTD
Cromwell House, Church Street, Princes Risborough,
Aylesbury, Bucks HP17 9AJ, UK

Series Editor: Barbara Adams

ISBN 0 85263 938 4

First published 1988

Set in 11 point Times and printed in Great Britain by
C. I. Thomas & Sons (Haverfordwest) Ltd
Press Buildings, Merlins Bridge, Haverfordwest, Dyfed

Contents

4

List of illustrations

Chronology

Palaeolithic	500,000 - 5500 BC	500,000 BC Lower Palaeolithic 100,000 BC Middle Palaeolithic 30,000 BC Upper Palaeolithic 10,000 - 5500 BC Epi-palaeolithic
Predynastic	5500 - 3050 BC 5500 - 4000 BC Lower Egypt Upper Egypt 4000 - 3500 BC Lower Egypt Upper Egypt 3500 - 3300 BC Lower Egypt Upper Egypt 3500 - 3050 BC Lower Egypt 3300 - 3150 BC Upper Egypt	 Fayum A, Merimda Badarian ?Omari A Amratian (Naqada I) ?Omari B Early Gerzean (Naqada II) Maadi Late Gerzean (Naqada II)
Protodynastic	3200 - 3050 BC	Naqada III (Late Gerzean)
Early Dynastic	3050 - 2613 BC	Dynasties I - II
Old Kingdom	2613 - 2181 BC	Dynasties III - VI
First Intermediate Period	2181 - 2040 BC	Dynasties VII - XI(1)
Middle Kingdom	2040 - 1782 BC	Dynasties XI(2) - XII
Second Intermediate Period	1782 - 1570 BC	Dynasties XIII - XVII
New Kingdom	1570 - 1070 BC	Dynasties XVIII - XX
Third Intermediate Period	1070 - 713 BC	Dynasties XXI - XXIV
Late Period	713 - 332 BC	Dynasties XXV - XXXI
Graeco-Roman Period	332 BC - AD 395	Ptolemies and Roman Emperors

Acknowledgements

Without the inspiration of working with the fine Predynastic collection amassed by Flinders Petrie at University College London, I would perhaps not have sustained a continued interest in this particular phase of Egypt's past. Among the living, I could not owe a greater debt to Professor Michael Allen Hoffman, who has enabled me to work on a modern excavation in Egypt where collaboration with members of the Hierakonpolis expedition has revitalised my involvement.

Mrs Joan Crowfoot Payne has for some years been my guide in matters concerning Predynastic Egypt and many other colleagues, such as Professor Fekri A. Hassan, have provided refreshing discussions about matters of mutual interest. Those who specifically helped with the production of this book were Mrs Angela P. Thomas of the Bolton Museum and Art Gallery, Professor Arthur F. Shore of the School of Archaeology and Oriental Studies, University of Liverpool, Dr Edward Brovarsky of the Boston Museum of Fine Arts and Dr A. Rosalie David of the Manchester University Museum. Miss Diane L. Holmes generously supplied an outline of procedures undertaken by lithic analysts.

Special thanks are due to Mrs Helena Jaeschke (Archaeoptyx Archaeological Drawing Services) who produced the drawings (except for figures 21 and 47). We worked closely together to devise illustrations that would encompass a wide range of artefacts and present them in a lucid way. Unless otherwise stated, all reproductions are copyright of the Department of Egyptology, University College London. The outline dynastic chronology is based on that of Dr William J. Murnane and acknowledgement is made to him and Penguin Books for its use here.

1
Introduction

The beginning of history is defined by Egyptologists as taking place at the time of the unification of Upper and Lower Egypt under one ruler and the beginning of the First Dynasty (3050 BC). A glance at the chronology at the beginning of this book will indicate the great length of time which preceded this historic period of which the monumental remains still exist. What came before established the fundamental basis of this civilisation, founded on the richness that the Nile produced, and the possibilities for advancement which resulted in a stable government and a socio-religious pattern which endured through many changes and vicissitudes down to the Roman period.

As in other parts of the world, the first few hundred thousand years of human occupation in Egypt was by stone age, or palaeolithic, hunting, fishing and food-gathering communities living along the river terraces of the Nile valley. From about 5000 BC the earliest agricultural communities were developing and already there were some differences between those in Upper and Lower Egypt. In Lower Egypt there were neolithic settlements around the Fayum Lake basin and at Merimda, which is near the south-western edge of the Delta. Both of these sites produced pottery, traces of houses and abundant signs of agriculture and the domestication of animals. In the Badarian culture of Upper Egypt the copper ore, malachite, was used to make glaze for beads and some objects were produced in the metal. By this stage of the fourth millennium BC the degree of social complexity and the knowledge of metallurgy had reached the phase in prehistoric development which is usually called the Predynastic in Egypt. It will be seen that many artefacts produced had already established a peculiarly Egyptian character, the styles of which were to continue through the next cultural phases into the early historic period.

Through the accidents of the Nile's alluvial deposition and selective exploration, less is known about the Predynastic cultures of Lower Egypt than those of Upper Egypt. The situation is gradually being rectified with the re-excavation of sites such as Maadi south of Cairo and work at Minshat Abu

Omar in the eastern Delta. It would seem that the later phases at Merimda are contemporary with Naqada I in the south and the town site of El Omari may be slightly later and therefore nearer to Naqada II. The large town site of Maadi, where copper working took place, is late Predynastic and Protodynastic in date. Artefacts found there indicate contacts with the Upper Egyptian people of the south and trade with Palestine-Syria. At Minshat Abu Omar the cemetery material is remarkably similar to that of the Naqada III period in Upper Egypt and the excavator has postulated a peaceful co-existence and gradual assimilation by the southerners. Tradition, however, based on Early Dynastic commemorative scenes and later texts, holds that the unification of Egypt resulted from expansionist and warlike policies of the successful late Predynastic, Upper Egyptian kingdom based on the site of Hierakonpolis. There is certainly archaeological evidence both there and elsewhere in Upper Egypt of a continued and steady increase in population and social complexity with the early appearance of a ruling class in a stratified society. As most of the early objects in museums come from the south, this book concentrates on the material culture of Upper Egypt and its evolution through the Predynastic.

In chapter 3 there is a description of the way in which pottery has been used as a relative dating tool (Sequence Dating or seriation) to reconstruct the outline of the development of the Predynastic in Upper Egypt. In recent times this framework has been augmented by the use of the carbon-14 radiochemical dating technique (see chapter 6) but there is still some controversy about the accuracy of the dates derived from this method, especially where they seem to conflict with the pattern derived from the seriated framework. There is no written evidence as there is in the historic period in Egypt when the dates of most of the dynasties of kings are known with a fair degree of accuracy and can be correlated with astronomical phenomena and events in nearby foreign lands. The prehistorian has to use the archaeological evidence to reconstruct the life style of the people whose remains are being studied. The products of a culture are the artefacts, the so-called material culture from which a way of life has to be inferred and even political events reconstructed. As the discovery of these artefacts is accidental there can always be disagreement about their interpretation because revision or complete reinterpretation can be necessary as new data becomes available. The accuracy of explanatory frameworks is tested by new results and fortunately the model set up by the early workers in Egyptian prehistory still seems to have general validity, although current work in the field is producing some exciting and elucidating results.

The framework of cultural phases given in the chronology and detailed in the description of Sequence Dating in chapter 3 has the Badarian culture pre-dating and overlapping with the Amratian, or Naqada I, culture which had artefact types continuing and expanding from the Badarian, increased use of copper, amulets, figurines, larger tombs and the first painted pottery. These were followed by the Gerzean, or Naqada II, culture when an expansion and diversity is especially evident in the flowering of arts and crafts and the size and design of tombs. The increase in population and the growth of towns were leading to the formation of the Upper Egyptian state. In the past there has been speculation about the last phase of the Predynastic, some authors insisting that it was part of the Gerzean, others making it a separate culture (Semainean). Now the consensus of opinion favours a period of transition of about 150 years from the end of the Gerzean to the unification of Egypt before the Early Dynastic, or Archaic, period. During this Naqada III, or Protodynastic, period there were Upper Egyptian kings reigning from Hierakonpolis and the pottery types certainly showed continuity from the Gerzean but also had a separate identity which in many cases is echoed in the First Dynasty.

Both the climate and the Predynastic custom of burying their dead in the dry desert sand have fortuitously preserved various kinds of artefact from Predynastic Egypt to which various chapters are devoted in this book. The main categories of objects, apart from pottery, are vessels in a variety of hard and soft stones; stone mace-heads; metal tools such as needles, chisels and adzes; metal jewellery such as bracelets and rings; flint tools and weapons, both exotic and utilitarian; ivory, pottery and stone human and animal figurines; ivory, stone, shell and glazed composition (faience) beads and amulets; slate cosmetic palettes; ivory, bone and shell spoons, dishes, combs, bracelets and hairpins; leather and textile clothes and containers; and baskets, resins and plant food remains. In the case of settlements, pottery sherds and stone tools are usually the most abundant finds, although some organic remains, particularly wooden posts and animal bones, can be salvaged by careful excavation. The Egyptians had already developed a system of belief and many of the small artefacts and the decorated pottery depict zoomorphic deities and prophylactic devices to protect and ward off evil.

There were totems and emblems of power which signify that a complex society was developing and its class structure and organisation made possible the increasing use of the many natural resources the Nile valley and its fringes have to offer, such as clay, ores, stone, animal and plant substances. The structure of society also created a demand for other goods and a trading network which reached beyond the borders of Egypt brought in luxury items and minerals which were unobtainable locally, as well as ideas and influences which may have provided an impetus for further development.

Apart from the inferences that can be drawn from studying the artefacts of this early period of ancient Egypt, it should not be forgotten that they can also be appreciated as objects in their own right. Whilst little from the Predynastic could be described as works of art, there is a simplicity and economy of line in the shapes and decorative devices which is not unpleasing. They are evocative of their time and the environment in which they were created and cannot be mistaken for anything produced elsewhere. In some ways they provide a closer link with the human beings who created them than the repetitious and often impersonal liturgies inscribed on later Egyptian temple walls.

1. General view of the Predynastic town in the desert at Hierakonpolis looking towards the cultivation. Free-standing Pleistocene silts, craters and sherd piles can be seen. (Photograph by Barbara Adams.)

2
Sources of material

Lower Egypt

The Predynastic sites excavated in Lower Egypt are predominantly settlements, whilst those in Upper Egypt are chiefly cemeteries. This imbalance is gradually being redressed as cemeteries are located in the Delta and further settlement sites are excavated in the south. In the north at the large site of Merimda, first excavated by Hermann Junker between 1928 and 1939 and more recently by Josef Eiwanger, the accumulated debris of the three phases of occupation reached a depth of over 2 metres (6 feet 7 inches). The oval houses and shelters in the upper levels were semi-subterranean with mud walls and probably wattle superstructures. The neolithic sites in the Fayum Oasis basin were first excavated by Gertrude Caton Thompson and Elinor Gardner in the 1920s and numerous grain silos and many hearths were found in the village areas during their excavations. Further investigations of this rich area have been undertaken in modern times by various expeditions, most notably those led by Boreslaw Ginter and Robert Wenke. At El Omari there were also round huts and at both main sites women and children were buried in the settlements, although a village near the main site had associated, separate cemeteries with burials beneath tumuli, but with no standard orientation of the bodies. Fernand Debono, who excavated El Omari in the 1940s, is still working on the material from the site. At the large site of Maadi, explored by Oswald Menghin and Amer Mustafa in the 1930s and in the 1980s by an Italo-Egyptian mission led by Alba Palmieri, there were subterranean storage cellars, oval huts and some rectangular houses with a palisade and ditch defence perimeter. The dead were not normally buried within the settlement at Maadi except for foetuses, infants and a few women. There were three associated cemeteries; in two the graves were roofed with stone slabs like dolmens and in the third, earlier cemetery they were simple oval pits in the soil. Most of the bodies were orientated with the head south and the face east.

Settlements

There are some settlements known in southern Egypt, at Hemamiya in Middle Egypt, in the Theban area at El-Tarif, Naqada and Koptos, and in the south at Hierakonpolis, near

Edfu. At Hemamiya there was a stratified occupation site in which the Gerzean and Amratian artefacts overlay the Badarian. In the Amratian levels a small village was excavated with nine circular structures which had mud mixed with stone fragments as foundations; one house contained a hearth. At El-Tarif, at the foot of the Theban hills, two dwellings which probably date to Naqada II were found in 1978 in the upper layer of a prehistoric settlement. These were rectangular, the largest 3.5 by 2.5 metres (11 feet 6 inches by 8 feet 3 inches), with slightly rounded corners and stone foundations. Four hearths, which all showed signs of charring, were arranged in a semicircle around the structures.

At Naqada, which was excavated by William Matthew Flinders Petrie and James Quibell in 1895, there are a number of settlement areas, much destroyed. The South Town, which contained rectangular mud-brick houses and part of a fortification wall possibly 2 metres (6 feet 7 inches) thick, dates to Naqada II. This site and other nearby settlements have been the subject of modern excavations conducted principally by Fekri Hassan. At Koptos, also excavated by Petrie early in his career, Predynastic flints were found beneath a later town and temple in a yellow clay mound, but no structures were recorded.

One of the major problems in the excavation of Predynastic settlement sites is the scattered, ruinous remains of horizontally stratified mud brick, often attacked by the *sebakh* diggers who used the material as fuel. The tell structures of Mesopotamia, where layers of occupation surmount each other and rise to form artificial hills, are non-existent in early Egypt. Thus the early excavators can be forgiven for inadequately reconstructing the architecture within these settlements. At Hierakonpolis, the Predynastic town on the desert edge covers a vast area of 4.5 ha (11 acres) and looks like a crater field with piles of sherds and stone around sand-filled depressions almost as far as the eye can see (figure 1).

During excavations at Hierakonpolis in 1979, led by Michael Hoffman, the fortuitous discovery was made of a house burnt down and therefore 'fossilised' (figure 2), with its associated kiln. The kiln consists of eight basins (once ten) in a roughly oval area with large, rectangular firedogs of straw-tempered pottery which had supported storage vessels. The kiln was funnelled, to take advantage of a north wind, and a change in the wind direction probably brought about the conflagration of the nearby house. The house itself is 4 by 3.5 metres (13 feet 2 inches by 11 feet 6 inches) and the semi-subterranean walls are built of mud bricks in

2. The rectangular, burnt mud-brick house at Hierakonpolis viewed from the entrance. There are traces of wood in the left corner; the hearth is on the right. (Photograph by Barbara Adams.)
3. Reconstruction of the burnt house at Hierakonpolis with mud-brick lower walls and a wood, reed and skin superstructure. The hearth is on the pedestal in the lower corner. (After Hoffman.)

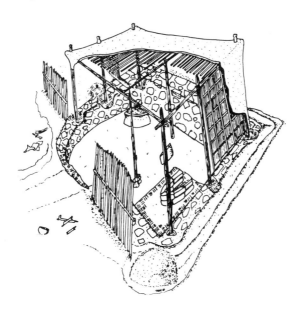

which pottery sherds are interspersed. There were wooden posts and an embedded storage jar *in situ,* and a hearth in the north-east corner. The superstructure was probably wattle and daub (see the reconstruction, figure 3), with a porch supported by posts. This dwelling and those around it were associated with fenced enclosures and outbuildings in a farmyard arrangement, and it succeeded similar earlier complexes. This must have been true of the entire town as it expanded from Amratian to Gerzean times, although later excavations nearer the valley have also revealed functional differentiation with an oval, open court surrounded by large post-holes marking the buildings of a possible Gerzean temple complex.

Prior to the 1978-9 excavations at El-Tarif and Hierakonpolis, the main evidence for rectangular houses being built in the Naqada II period was the pottery model house found in a grave at El Amrah and now in the British Museum. This has a doorway depicted beneath a lintel at one end and, from its height of 10 cm (4 inches), an estimate that the dimensions of the original house were 8 by 5.7 metres (26 feet 3 inches by 18 feet 8 inches) has been made. It seems that the evolution of houses was paralleled by the evolution in the shape of graves from round to rectangular.

In addition to the large town on the edge of the desert, Hierakonpolis also had seasonal camps for flock herders and pottery kiln sites to service the cemeteries in the Great Wadi to the west of the Nile valley. In the alluvial area there is the ruin of a later city, anciently called *Nekhen,* within mud-brick walls of the New Kingdom. It has been known since the start of the twentieth century that the town was important from before the First Dynasty and that there were artefacts of Predynastic date beneath it. This was dramatically confirmed in 1984 when core samples revealed a 3.5 metre (13 foot 2 inch) accumulation of Predynastic deposits beneath the First Dynasty levels, possibly dating back to Naqada I. Excavations using sludge pumps to deal with the saturated mud revealed a rectangular structure with associated pottery of Naqada II/III and a thick, possible enclosure wall of mud brick. At Hierakonpolis, as at other sites, it seems that not only did desert-edge occupation give way to town dwelling in the valley towards the late Predynastic when Nile floods and their effects had reduced, but that there were villages from earlier times in the alluvium, probably on levees left by river meanders, one of which developed into the city of Nekhen. It seems that in the early Gerzean, Naqada was the centre of an embryo Upper Egyptian state and, as the culture spread south, Hierakonpolis took over as the capital.

Cemeteries
The spread of cemeteries along the valley edge is somewhat dependent on date. For instance, the Badarian seems to extend only from Badari, near Asyut in Middle Egypt, to possibly Hierakonpolis in the south (no cemeteries), whilst the Amratian (Naqada I) stretches from near Badari in Middle Egypt to south of the first cataract into Nubia; the type site is El Amrah near Abydos. Gerzean (Naqada II) sites are known from the Delta to Lower Nubia; the type site is at Gerzeh near the Fayum basin. An old view, based on negative evidence, held that the Gerzean spread south from the Delta, but it is now believed that both Naqada I and II originated in the general area of modern Luxor and spread north and south. Within this long geographical area quite a few cemeteries have been discovered and only the larger sites can be mentioned in any detail. The looted necropolis at Abusir el Melek in the north near Gerzeh and the Fayum was excavated by Georg Möller before 1914, but his findings were published only after his death, by Alexander Scharff. It produced artefacts similar to those of Naqada II and III in the south, but also different types with affinities to Palestinian prototypes, perhaps a purer form of the culture. Work in the 1980s at Minshat Abu Omar in the Delta, directed by Dietrich Wildung, has disclosed 340 Naqada II, III and Early Dynastic simple graves with the bodies orientated head north and face west. In Middle Egypt there are the cemeteries of Matmar, Mostagedda, Badari and Qau el Kebir, all excavated by Guy Brunton in the 1920s and 1930s. Naqada and Ballas, above Thebes in Upper Egypt, produced nearly three thousand graves and the contents of these and those from the cemeteries at Diospolis Parva (Hu, Abadiyeh) near Abydos were used by Petrie to formulate his famous Sequence Dating system (see chapter 3). Also near Abydos there are the important cemeteries of Mahasna and El Amrah, and that of Naga ed-Dêr. Below Thebes there is Armant, which was well excavated by Oliver Myers in the 1930s, and Gebelein, a sadly looted ruin from which many objects found their way on to the antiquities market (figure 34). Further south near Edfu there is Hierakonpolis, or the Kom el-Ahmar, and there are other sites in this region such as El-Kab, which was studied by a Belgian mission in the 1970s and 1980s. This expedition not only found further graves of a Naqada III cemetery first discovered by Quibell in 1897 within the mud-brick New Kingdom town

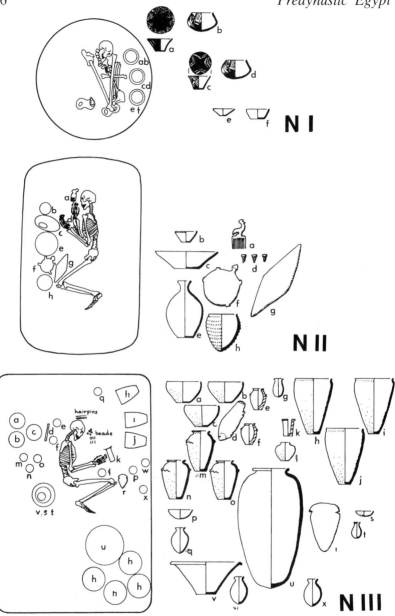

4. Typical layouts of Naqada I (Amratian), Naqada II (Gerzean) and Naqada III (Protodynastic) graves showing the evolution in size and shape and the disposition and type of grave goods.

enclosure *(Nekheb)*, but also very interesting early graffiti incised into the rocks of the eastern desert wadi.

Within the cemeteries there was an evolution in the shape, size and contents of the graves as well as in the types of artefacts deposited in them (figure 4). During the Badarian period graves were oval or circular and the bodies were often wrapped in goat skins or mats, possibly in twig boxes, in a loosely contracted position with their hands before the face and their legs bent to the chest, as if in a foetal position. The grave goods were placed outside the mat bundles. The graves of Naqada I were not essentially different from those of the Badarian, the circular graves being thought the earliest (figure 4, NI). They mostly contained polished red or white cross-lined pottery and exotic items such as ivory and bone combs and pottery figurines. In Naqada II the graves became bigger and were often lined with wood and roofed with sticks or matting, but the body was still in the contracted position. A pattern for the disposal of the grave goods was emerging which became established by late Naqada II. The smaller pots, hairpins, jewellery, slate cosmetic palettes and stone vessels tended to be clustered around the head and the large storage vessels which started to appear then were placed near the feet. In figure 5 the size of an important transitional Naqada I/II grave, excavated in the large cemetery 2 km (1¼ miles) along the Great Wadi at Hierakonpolis in 1980, is indicated by the presence of the excavator within it looking at what remained of the objects on its base. Sadly this particular tomb (number 3), nearly 2 metres deep by 2.50 metres long (6 feet 7 inches by 8 feet 3 inches) and 1.80 metres wide (5 feet 11 inches) at the base, had been completely disturbed and all that was left *in situ* was a basket containing reed arrow shafts, a twig bier on which rested the bones of a goat and a black and white porphyry disc mace-head. Fortunately the sherds scattered throughout the fill were recovered and from them nine black-topped red vessels and eight straw-tempered vessels were reconstructed (figure 9), but there was nothing to suggest their original emplacement. There were also numerous fragments of leather, twigs and matting which suggested the presence of a lashed box around the occupant, who is thought to be male from the partially reconstructed skull.

In many cemeteries there was differentiation in the size and quality of graves in the later Predynastic periods, which is one indication of the formation of a society with an emerging aristocratic class. There also seems to be a puzzling disproportion

5. Tomb 3 at Hierakonpolis with the excavator, Carter Lupton of the Milwaukee Museum, viewing the disc mace-head, goat bones and fragments of baskets *in situ* on the base. (Photograph by Barbara Adams.)

between population estimates based on settlement size and cemetery grave counts in the few places where these are comparable, possibly indicating that the very lowest class of society was not accorded proper burial, or that many cemeteries have been destroyed. At Naqada, the large brick-lined tombs with semi-partition walls were grouped in a separate Gerzean cemetery. The most famous tomb of this type at Hierakonpolis, in a cemetery south of the Predynastic town, had a plastered wall painted with scenes of men, boats and desert animals in red, white and black on a yellow background. By Naqada III, many graves were entirely rectangular and pottery box coffins of straw-tempered ware were used to contain the contracted body in larger graves. There was also an increase in multiple burials in smaller tombs and a decrease in individuals in larger tombs, indicating that only an élite minority was accorded larger tombs in special areas. In the case of the Protodynastic kings at Hierakonpolis and Abydos the mud-brick lined tombs became very much larger with plank roofs and wooden posts around the tombs supporting earth superstructures. Richness, as defined by the number of objects in a grave, was also confined to about 10 per cent of the graves in a wide range of cemeteries through Naqada II/III times.

During the Badarian the head of the body usually pointed to the north and faced east. A long period of orthodoxy followed in Naqada I/II in which it became standard practice at most sites to place the body facing west with the head pointing south. During Naqada III and the First Dynasty there was a partial reversion to the earlier fashion for head north and face east, which perhaps had something to do with the mortuary cult, although it may be indicative of the greater contact with Lower Egyptian practice.

From this survey of the development of the tomb in the Predynastic it can be seen that by the time of the unification there was already an established format for the size and shape of graves of the upper echelons of society. These brick-lined sepulchres evolved smoothly into the mastaba tombs of the Early Dynastic period which had chambers in the substructures and super-structures to contain the ever increasing equipment required in the afterlife, a trend which began a thousand years before.

3
Pottery

Pottery is the most abundant and durable of the cultural remains from antiquity preserved in Egypt. Any visitor to the necropolis at Saqqara near Cairo can testify to the sea of pottery sherds over which his feet crunch on the desert surface, representing the debris of four thousand years of human activity. As pottery is breakable with a somewhat limited life and its production relatively easy and subject to prevailing fashion, its analysis can be used as a tool in relative dating. In the historic period there are often inscriptions in dated contexts to which the associated pottery can be linked and in this way a framework of date ranges for the types can be produced. In no other period is pottery analysis as relevant as in the Predynastic, where there is no historic framework to provide this link because of the absence of a written language. Flinders Petrie, working at the end of the nineteenth century, was a pioneer in the field of archaeological ceramics, both from Egypt and Palestine, and the first Egyptologist who, like General Pitt-Rivers in England, learned to 'read the pottery' from the sites.

At the time of Petrie's initial work on the Predynastic assemblages from cemeteries, there were no excavated, stratified village sites with sequences of levels which could be correlated by means of pottery sherds to give an archaeological progression. Instead, Petrie first identified the distinctive pottery types and then devised a system of relative dating, or seriation, termed Sequence Dating, based on the increase and decrease in the frequencies of these types and the other objects in the graves. Thus a chronological and typological framework was established for the Upper Egyptian Predynastic cultures which is still the basis for work today.

The hand-made pottery types identified at that time are as follows. The black-topped vessels, or B class, are made of black-to-red firing Nile silt with a polished red surface and a blackened area below the rim, which was probably produced by placing the vessel upside down in reducing organic material immediately after firing. Closely allied are the polished red vessels, or P class, which have the same surface treatment but lack the blackened rims and interiors. There is an all-black polished ware (in Petrie's F for fancy class) which has the same fabric and surface treatment as the polished red pottery. Petrie's

6. A black-topped brown Badarian pottery bowl with rippled decoration over the surface impressed into the leather-hard clay before firing; from a grave at Badari. (UC.9011.)

strangely named white cross-lined, or C class, is polished red pottery which has the addition of painted decoration in white. The fabric of all these Nile silt wares contains a very fine micaceous sand, but it is not certain whether this is an added temper or a constituent of the alluvial clay. There appears to have been regional variation in the use of temper, but it seems that animal dung, which contains fine chaff, was added to give body. It is not always easy to determine whether a slip was applied to the surface of the pots because they were polished with a pebble at the leather-hard stage before firing. Patterns of this burnishing can be observed, usually horizontally around the rim and vertically on the body of the pots.

Another Nile silt fabric is that described as rough, or R class, by Petrie. It is a coarse straw-tempered pottery which has proved to be the utilitarian ware of settlements but did not appear in any quantity until the second phase of the Predynastic sequence in the graves (Naqada II), as if in the earlier phase only the 'best' tableware was deemed good enough for the dead, whilst later quantity was as relevant. These pots have no surface treatment, apart from smoothing and the occasional incised design, and the shapes are shared with other categories, particularly the P and L classes. The last Nile silt group set up by Petrie includes the

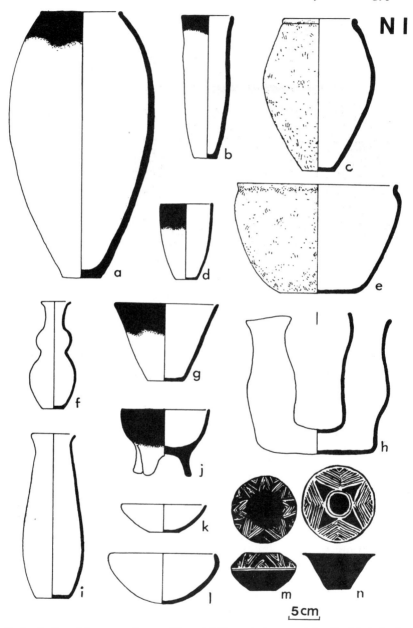

7. A selection of the corpus shapes of Naqada I (Amratian) pottery (after Petrie): (a, b, d, g, j) black-topped red (Petrie's B class); (c, e) straw-tempered (Petrie's R class); (f, h, i, k, l) polished red (Petrie's P class); (m, n) white cross-lined (Petrie's C class).

8. A black-topped pot in the form of an open-mouthed fish, probably early Naqada II. (UC.2965.)

Nubian pottery (N class), which is usually fired black-to-brown, often with incised geometric designs.

A fine calcareous clay (marl) from the soft shale in the desert wadis was used to manufacture the D, W and L classes which fired orange/pink at lower temperatures and buff or greenish cream at higher temperatures. The surfaces were smoothed, sometimes slipped and, in the case of the D, or decorated, class, had designs in an ochre paint of plum-red hue. Petrie defined another group as W class or 'wavy-handled', which today is considered a misnomer because its definition strictly has nothing to do with the fabric or overall surface treatment, but refers to the form of the pottery which has two applied wavy handles in relief. The presumed sequential change in the wavy-handled types, shown in figure 13, was the basis of Petrie's Sequence Dating.

Petrie's L, or late, class is an unacceptable grouping of pottery which includes various fabrics and surface treatments (straw-tempered wares, marl wares, red-slipped wares, and so on) linked by their chronological position at the end of the Predynastic sequence.

The selected typical pottery corpuses here (figures 7, 10 and 15) are grouped in the major divisions of the Predynastic sequence which were established by Petrie. Within the classes Petrie further divided the pottery by form from the most open

9. Two black-topped red jars and a streak-burnished brown jar reconstructed from the fragments found in Tomb 3 at Hierakonpolis, Naqada I-II. (Photograph by Barbara Adams.)

types, such as bowls, to the most closed, such as bottles. The first group (figure 7) indicates some of the pottery types typical of the Amratian, or Naqada I, period and includes the black-topped, polished red, white cross-lined and rough Nile silt wares as jars, bottles, dishes and bowls. The next group (figure 10) covers the Gerzean, or Naqada II, period and shows the continuation of the black-topped and polished red vessels with changes in shape, the expansion of the R (straw-tempered) types and the introduction of the black polished Nile silt ware and the plum-red painted calcareous ware as well as the plain types. The next corpus extract (figure 13) gives Petrie's version of the evolution of wavy-handled types from the earliest squat rounded jars with exaggerated handles, thought to copy Palestinian prototypes (a, b), through the tapering Egyptian versions (c-g) to the final vestigial wavy lines of the last phase of the Predynastic (h-j) and the Early Dynastic cylinder vases (k, l). The last selected assemblage here (figure 15) illustrates Protodynastic, or Naqada III, pottery and covers the continuation of the P and R classes, the simplified decorated wares of this phase and the introduction of the L class; the black-topped vessels no longer appear.

For ease of comprehension the fabric of the figured pottery

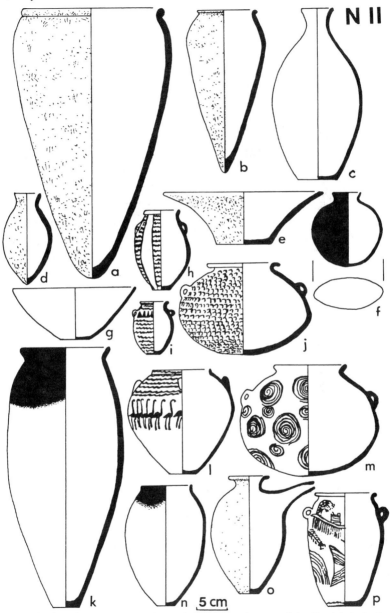

10. A selection of corpus shapes of Naqada II (Gerzean) pottery (after Petrie): (a, b, d, e) straw-tempered (Petrie's R class); (c, g) polished red (Petrie's P class); (f) black polished (Petrie's F class); (h, i, j, l, m, n, p) plum-red painted buff/pink marl (Petrie's D class); (k, n) black-topped red (Petrie's B-class); (o) smooth buff/pink marl (Petrie's L class).

11. Decorated pot in the form of a boat from grave B182 at Abadiyeh. (UC. 10805.)

12. Pot in the form of a bird (head missing) with a painted row of birds on the body, from a Naqada II grave in the fort cemetery at Hierakonpolis. (Courtesy of the School of Archaeology and Oriental Studies, University of Liverpool, E3036.)

types has been indicated in these drawings, so that the polished red surface is seen as plain, the black-topped red as black on plain, the white cross-lined on red polished as white on black, the R or straw-tempered ware as stippled and the L, D and W classes (marl wares) as more lightly stippled to distinguish them from the Nile silt types. With this shading in mind it is possible to see the virtue of a revision of Petrie's classes proposed by a Canadian called Walter Federn in 1945 and more recently espoused by Winifred Needler. In this Federn retained Petrie's B, P, C, R, N and W classes, but added a B1 to cover bowls that are polished black on the interior and red outside, and a B-P to extract the black polished wares from Petrie's fancy group, thereby demolishing it. He then usefully broke down the unsatisfactory late class into S for smooth to cover the calcareous plain pottery, usually large storage vessels, P1 to cover a polished red surface

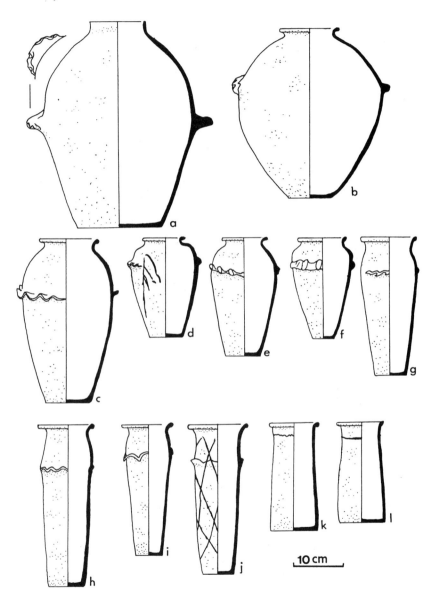

13. The evolution of the wavy-handled pottery types as envisaged by Petrie from the full-bodied jars (a and b) which copied Palestinian shapes through the typical Gerzean shapes (c, d, e, f, g) to the Protodynastic (h, i, j) and Early Dynastic (k and l) cylinders with vestigial wavy lines.

treatment on S (marl fabric) and P2 for half-polished bowls of similar fabric with a red slip or wash over the interior and just below the rim on the exterior. This type is indicated on figure 15a with a broken line shading below the rim; it has proved to be a chronological marker for the transition between Naqada II and III both in whole pots seriated from graves and in quantified sherds from the settlement beneath the city at Hierakonpolis.

As well as refinements of Petrie's divisions of pottery types, there have been various re-workings of his seriation method, which was achieved in 1899 without benefit of modern technology after shuffling and sorting slips marked with the pottery types for nine hundred graves selected from the four thousand excavated at Hu, Abadiyeh (Diospolis Parva), Naqada and Ballas. Petrie then assigned stages to cover their inception, flourishing and degradation so that, after leaving a space for earlier material, the Predynastic had a range from Sequence Date (SD) 30-39 for the Amratian (Naqada I), SD 40-52 for the Gerzean (Naqada II) and SD 54-79 for what Petrie called the Semainean (Naqada III). His later work at Abydos and Tarkhan took the Sequence Dates, SD 77-84, into the First and Second Dynasties. All other categories of objects were fitted into the Sequence Dating framework, which is meant to indicate the order of development and the relation of objects to each other and not to be a measurement of

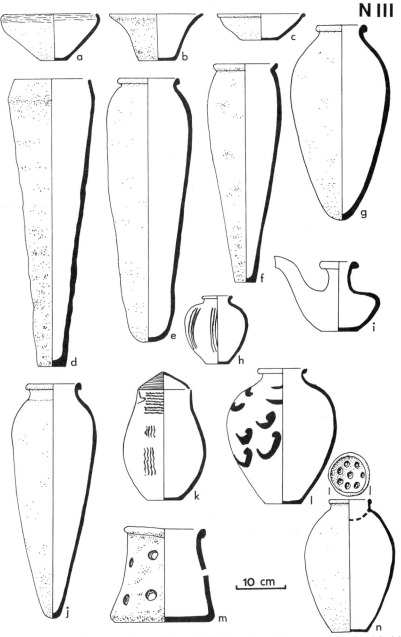

15. A selection of corpus shapes of Naqada III (Protodynastic) pottery (after Petrie): (a) buff/pink marl ware bowl with red slipped interior and exterior rim; (b, d, f, m) straw-tempered (Petrie's R class); (c, e, g, j) buff/pink marl (Petrie's L class); (i) polished red (Petrie's P class); (h, k, l) buff/pink painted marl ware (Petrie's D class); (n) marl ware jar with integral strainer in mouth (Petrie's L class).

time; therefore the Sequence Date numbers do not necessarily have the same values.

Whilst Petrie's achievement remains innovative and classic, the most accepted refinement in recent years has been that of the German, Werner Kaiser, who seriated the pottery from the cemetery excavated by Myers at Armant and produced a sequence of further sub-divisions: Naqada I (= SD 30-38), Naqada II a, b (= SD 38/40-45), Naqada II c, d (= SD 40/45-63) and Naqada III (= SD 63-80). He also showed that Petrie's reliance on wavy-handled pottery for Sequence Dating was unsound, so that SD 40-80 are dubious. There is still some controversy about which king is accepted as the first of a united Egypt, so that the beginning of the First Dynasty can fluctuate between SD 77 and 80, and it is obvious that there is some overlap between Naqada III and Dynasty I types, but overall the refined divisions of the Upper Egyptian cultural sequence have gained wide acceptance. Further confirmation was produced in a computerised seriation of the pottery from a cemetery at El Amrah by Barry Kemp in 1982 which defined the three major temporal groups and suggested a later break between I and II than Petrie set, and a sub-division within group II, none of which clashes with the scheme of stages, or *Stufen,* worked out by Kaiser.

Gertrude Caton Thompson was another pioneer who brought sherd studies into Egyptian archaeology when she excavated the stratified village settlement of Hemamiya in Middle Egypt in the 1920s and confirmed the phases of the Predynastic set up by Petrie. She and Guy Brunton also identified another cultural assemblage from the settlement and a cemetery at Badari which they termed the Badarian. The pottery of this group is similar to that of the neolithic cultures of Lower Nubia and to the succeeding Amratian, including black-topped Nile silt vessels with a characteristic ripple burnish over the brown surface which are among the finest pottery ever produced in the Nile valley (figure 6). Other artefacts are prototypes of those which continue into Naqada I and II. The Badarian was found beneath the Amratian and Gerzean levels at Hemamiya, therefore Petrie had also been correct in allowing a space for cultures to precede SD 30.

Modern analyses of pottery from the settlement sites being excavated require that whole assemblages be studied and defined and there are no convenient boundaries provided by the contents of one tomb, or a limited cemetery area. In the case of the site with which this author is most familiar, at Hierakonpolis in Upper Egypt, the quantity of the Predynastic pottery sherds scattered over the desert is simply staggering and produces a sense of wonder at the production of this indestructible material by early Egyptian potters. A system of sherd analysis has been set up there which has fabric or ware divisions very similar to the groups described above: I = straw-tempered (R); II = plum-red (B, P); III = grit-tempered (R); IV = straw- and stone-tempered (R); V = crushed calcium carbonate (L, W, D). The pottery is further sub-divided according to the part of the vessel from which it comes and the general shape classes are defined (dishes, bowls, large and small storage jars, bottles, vases). Rims and bases are then used to build up a shape typology and details of surface treatment such as painting, slipping or burnishing are added. These observations can be coded and vast quantities of sherds (over 350,000 from one part of the Predynastic settlement) can be recorded for computer analysis. The results obtained are corre-lated with the excavated archaeological units and strata, which can give an indication of functional areas from the frequency of certain types, and the earlier corpuses set up from the whole pots which were mostly derived from tombs. The ceramicist on a modern excavation not only needs a knowledge of the established fabric and corpus types and the revised systems, but also an ability to sort, quantify, code and record the masses of sherds that a day's digging can produce from even a modest excavation quadrant of 10 metres (33 feet), as well as the application to spot the potential joins in sherds from closed units such as graves.

There are further modern analytical devices available in the study of pottery. Of these, thermoluminescence (the emission of photons of visible light from electrons recombining with atoms when material is heated) is measurable in pottery because TL begins to accumulate again when pottery is fired above 600 C (1112 F) and can be measured on re-firing to estimate the length of time that has elapsed. The technique has been used to confirm that some suspect painted pots are Naqada II in date but were painted and re-fired in modern times. It has also been used to date sherds from the stratified site of Hemamiya and the date ranges given suggest that not only did the Badarian have a long time span from perhaps as early as 5500 BC, but it also seems to have continued and overlapped with the Amratian to 3800 BC. X-ray fluorescence and neutron activation analysis can be used to identify the elements present in an artefact in great detail, which then enables the sediment source to be located; this has

important implications in the consideration of pottery production
centres, foreign imports and trading patterns.

Pottery sherds were also re-used in antiquity. The Badarians
obviously prized their rippled bowls and drilled the edges of
broken sherds so that they could reconstruct the broken pots by
inserting wet thongs and letting them dry to pull the sherds
together. Sherds lying about the settlements were picked up and
drilled to make spindle whorls and some of them were probably
sketch pads for early artists (see figure 30). Others were used in
construction and as general scraping tools. The vandals who came
to despoil the cemeteries found that a smashed pot provided a
useful selection of digging tools to clear the graves and the sherds
so used have bevelled edges which makes pottery reconstruction
even more difficult.

4
Stone and metal working

Stone

Rare stone vases have been found in plundered cemeteries of the Badarian period, and from Naqada I they proliferated with an expanding variety of shapes and range of stone. This perhaps coincides with the perfection of metallurgy which produced the copper tools useful in working the intractable materials together with hard stone drills, a wet quartz sand abrasive and an abundance of patience. The stones came from the Nile valley and from the hills of the eastern desert in reach of the Wadi Hammamat, an ancient route to the Red Sea and a source of minerals.

Simple jars with flat bases were made of basalt in Naqada I and they may be copies of Badarian ivory vases (figure 16a, b); similar shapes were found at Merimda in Lower Egypt. Another popular early shape also made in hard basalt was the footed base, sometimes with two small perforated handles beneath the rim in which strings were inserted for suspension (figure 16c, d). It has been suggested these originated in Mesopotamia, where the shape was known, but the variety of stone was lacking, whereas it could be obtained from the southern Egyptian quarries at Aswan. Occasionally this shape was made in black (F class) pottery.

A typical shape of stone vessel in Naqada II was the squat jar with tubular perforated handles and a flat rim (figure 16e). Large examples of this bulbous shape were manufactured in the red and white breccia of Upper Egypt, which is a difficult stone to work as the igneous inclusions are often not well cemented in the matrix (figure 18). Nevertheless, smooth even surfaces were ground and the type was often copied in the decorated marl pottery (figure 10j, m) with the painting imitating the markings on the stone. Another typical Naqada II, or Gerzean, shape is the taller jar with perforated tubular handles (figure 16f, g) which sometimes had a low, indistinct ring base. This was manufactured in a variety of stones such as porphyry, limestone, serpentine, calcite, breccia and diorite. These were cosmetic containers placed in rich graves and sometimes the handles and rims were overlaid with beaten gold foil (figure 17). This type of cosmetic vase included examples with wavy handles copying pottery shapes and some in the form of animals, particularly frogs which were often made in an appropriate green stone such as serpentine. The basic shape of

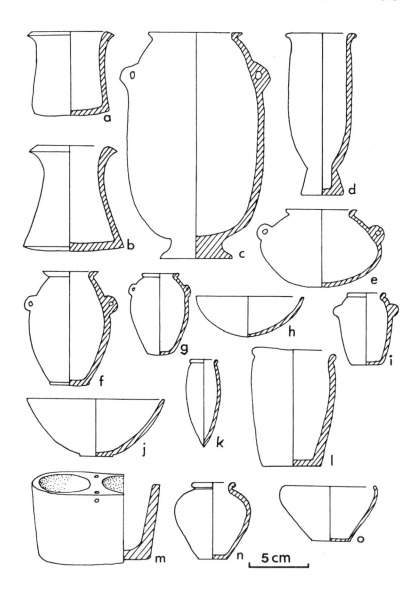

16. Stone vase shapes: (a-d) Naqada I; (e-h, j, k) Naqada II; (i, l, m-o) Naqada III. (After Petrie.)

17. Two Gerzean stone vases with tubular handles on the shoulders; the serpentine vase on the left has its rim and handles covered with gold foil, the vase on the right is breccia. (UC.15630 and UC.15637.)

this vase continued into Naqada III and the First Dynasty in a simplified form (figure 16i) connected with the cylinder vases that were then becoming popular (figure 16l). Other small vases are linked to the evolution of pottery shapes (figure 16k, n). The quality of the stone vase industry declined generally in Naqada III with the few finer vases being confined to élite cemeteries, but there was a resurgence in the Early Dynastic period when the political climate was more settled. Production increased and some exquisite examples were made for élite use while pottery continued to be generally utilitarian.

Bowls appeared in a wide variety of shapes and echoed pottery types, so that the plain bowls (figure 16h) date to Naqada II, whilst those with incurved rims (figure 16o) are, like the pottery bowls of the same shape, dated to Naqada III and the First Dynasty. Sometimes stone was used to make vases in the form of boxes and in Naqada III these often had drilled circular compartments (figure 16m). Examples of these were found in a large deposit of votive objects of Protodynastic and Early Dynastic date in the temple at Hierakonpolis.

Stone was also used for tools and weapons. The maces of hard

18. Large globular Gerzean vase made of breccia clearly showing the igneous inclusions in the stone. (UC.15587.)

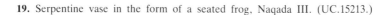

19. Serpentine vase in the form of a seated frog, Naqada III. (UC.15213.)

stones such as black and white porphyry (figure 23), calcite (still called alabaster by some Egyptologists) and hard limestone were weapons, symbols of power and possibly had ceremonial connotations from the earliest times. The disc mace-head with a central perforation (figure 20d), one of which was found in a grave at El Amrah with its wooden shaft partially intact, dates to Naqada I and early Naqada II. A collection of these disc maces, with many more pear-shaped types, was placed in the deposit at Hierakonpolis, perhaps collected from very early offerings in the temple. The pear-shaped, or piriform, mace-head entered in Naqada II and a famous commemorative palette depicts Narmer, an Upper Egyptian Protodynastic king, using one to smite his enemy. Thereafter it continues to be depicted in use by the Pharaoh in reliefs until the Ptolemaic period, in the same pose, held above the heads of captives who are grasped firmly by the hair. The shaft of a pear-shaped mace-head found in a grave in Nubia had gold ribbing imitating the binding cords of a flexible shaft. This example and the early depictions suggest that when the maces were used as weapons, rather than ceremonially, they were attached to a leather thong, for if the mace was used effectively any slender wooden shaft would break on impact. By Protodynastic times it is certain that the pear-shaped mace-head had important ceremonial connotations. Large examples from Hierakonpolis depict the early kings Scorpion and Narmer in relief, and one of the decorated ivories from the great deposit shows three large mace-heads mounted on ribbed columns with animals in procession in front of them.

By Naqada I pieces of flint were flaked to produce the fine knives which have been found in cemeteries. The classic shapes of this phase were the bifacially flaked, large rhombic knife (figure 20a) and the fishtail knife with concave end (figure 20b) which by Naqada II had evolved to a V shape (figure 20c). One of these fishtails was found in a grave at Naqada with fragments of its original hafting of cord at the pointed end, and pottery models with the fork tips painted red and the haft end black came from a grave at Hierakonpolis. Their purpose is not certain but they were probably the ancestors of the instrument used in the later ritual of 'opening the mouth' of the deceased. The early bifacially flaked comma-shaped knife (figure 20g) of Naqada I led to the meticulously flaked knives of Naqada II and III which were left ground on one side and ripple-flaked from each long edge to the centre on the other (figure 20h). Several of these knives, with elaborately decorated ivory handles, depicting scenes which have

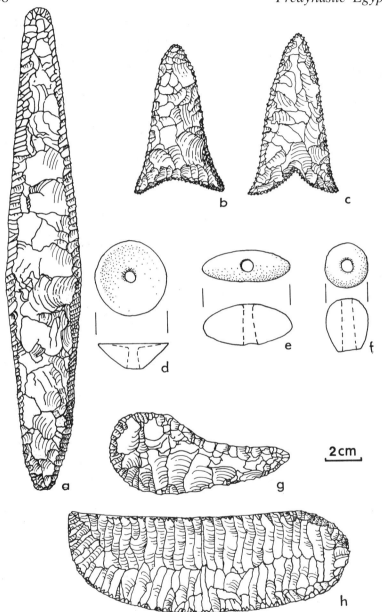

2cm

20. Fancy flint types and mace-heads: (a) rhomboidal bifacial knife; (b, c) Naqada I and II fishtail knives; (d) disc mace-head; (e) hammer mace-head; (f) pear-shaped mace-head; (g, h) comma-shaped bifacial knives. (After Brunton, Arkell and Needler.)

been discussed in debates on the unification of Egypt, have turned up on the antiquities market and in one or two graves. The fact that these elaborate tools are scarce in settlement sites and are standardised in form from cemeteries like Gerzeh in the north to those in Nubia has led to the suggestion that they were made by specialists at one or two places and then traded along the Nile valley. Replication of these fine knives has been undertaken in modern times, most notably by Peter Kelterborn. The technique was also used in ancient times to produce works of art such as the bifacially worked hippopotamus from a cemetery at Hierakonpolis (figure 22).

There was a utilitarian, localised Predynastic flint industry in the settlements which, like ceramics, is now receiving more attention as a result of more thorough excavation techniques. In the past it was common, even on well conducted excavations like those of Caton Thompson, for excavators to retain particular artefacts for museum collections. This obviously led to a bias towards the bifacial and ripple-flaked tools and perhaps created an artificial view of a settlement's tool assemblage if the rest of the material was not properly recorded. Nowadays all the material that results from flint-knapping is collected from an excavation unit, just as all the sherds are recovered. The lithic analyst then sets to work to sort the resulting masses of flint fragments into categories which are tabulated to give the number (frequency) and percentage of each category. This will immediately indicate the nature of the technology at the site and show from the percentage of cores and debitage, or pieces struck from a core or tool, if it was a locality where the tools were actually made and what type they were. Further analyses can then be made on the tools themselves, which are chiefly retouched blades and flakes, to divide them into types such as burins, endscrapers, side-scrapers, planes, perforators, sickle blades, axes, knives and arrowheads. A basic tool typology for the Predynastic (formulated by Diane Holmes) is shown in figure 21. Unfortunately the purpose of most of the tools is unknown, but specific technologies of tool manufacture can sometimes be ascertained. Sickle blades usually have serrated edges which still bear the silica gloss caused by cutting the plant stems; scrapers were probably used to prepare animal skins. The detailed study of flint working from earlier and present-day excavations can highlight the differences and similarities in domestic tool technology at various Predynastic settlement sites of comparable date. For instance, it confirms that the universal expansion of blade

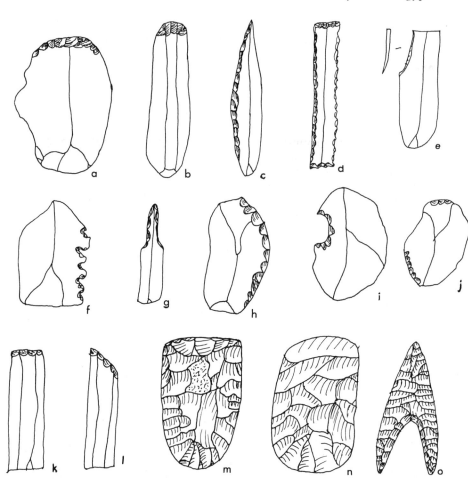

21. Flint types: (a) endscraper on flake; (b) endscraper on blade; (c) backed blade; (d) sickle blade; (e) burin with spall; (f) denticulate; (g) perforator; (h) sidescraper; (i) notch; (j) retouched piece; (k) straight truncation; (l) oblique truncation; (m) plane; (n) axe; (o) arrowhead. (After Diane Holmes.)

technology was in Naqada II, as was noted by earlier authors. It also reveals that axes were used during Amratian and early Gerzean times in the Naqada region but Hierakonpolis, whilst sharing scraper, burin and denticulate types with Naqada, lacks axes and has microdrills and winged drills instead, as well as an abundance of biface thinning flakes. This is obviously indicative of the specialised nature of activities in each of these areas,

Hierakonpolis perhaps being a centre for the manufacture of fine flints, beads, amulets and stone vases in Naqada II.

Metal

It is possible that the technique of glazing steatite beads with a glaze coloured by the green copper ore, malachite, led to the discovery of metallic copper by the Egyptians. Malachite was certainly used for this purpose in the Badarian period and the raw lumps were even ground on cosmetic palettes as eye make-up. At this time it was probably obtained from the mountains east of the Nile. In the Early Dynastic period the Egyptians mounted expeditions to obtain turquoise from the Sinai peninsula, where the goddess Hathor was the miners' patron, 'the Lady of the Turquoise'. Inscriptions record that copper ores were obtained from this source in the Old Kingdom. Copper tools were first attested in the graves at Badari — a couple of beads and a rod, both of hammered copper. Metal artefacts were also scarce in Naqada I graves, the looped pin for garment fastening being the most frequent, but this new material was probably the most attractive to plunderers, so there is, therefore, a negative bias from the cemeteries and so far the settlement sites have not produced evidence of copper working in the Amratian. There is no doubt, however, that metallurgy was developing in the early Predynastic because of the variety of copper, silver and gold tools and jewellery which has been recovered from the Gerzean

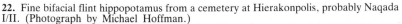

22. Fine bifacial flint hippopotamus from a cemetery at Hierakonpolis, probably Naqada I/II. (Photograph by Michael Hoffman.)

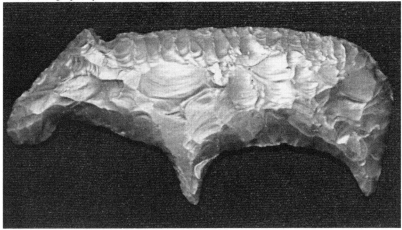

23. Black and white porphyry disc mace-head from Tomb 3 at Hierakonpolis. (Photograph by Barbara Adams.)

24. Silver and copper adzes from the cemetery at Naqada. (UC.5477, UC.5437.)

25. Two copper bracelets with punched decoration, a copper ring and a tubular copper bead from graves at Naqada, Gerzean. (UC.5067, UC.5069, UC.5063, UC.5066.)

cemeteries, despite the fact that these graves were often attacked by grave robbers and the metal objects were vulnerable to the ravages of time.

Copper was cast and then hammered to make tools such as axes and adzes (figure 24) and, more rarely, copper dagger blades have survived with midribs and rivet holes near the haft. A similar dagger in silver with an ivory handle came from a Naqada II grave at El Amrah. This metal is always rarer as it is not found in the native state in Egypt and it is thought the ore was imported from north Syria. It corrodes more easily than copper or gold, but it has been found used for beads and spoons in the Predynastic. Copper was also used for smaller tools such as chisels, needles and spatulas (figure 26). The harpoons (figure 26) of copper were copied in bone and ivory (figure 27) and are found in both tombs and settlement sites. Copper was also, no doubt, made into saws and drills for wood and stone working, but no Predynastic examples of these have been discovered. Rings and bracelets of beaten and decorated copper were also made (figure 25) and it was twisted into wire and used for various attachments and fittings.

Much later, Egypt was known as the land of gold, much as legend had it that the streets of London were so paved, and the

26. A small copper adze, a silver spatula and a copper single-barbed harpoon from graves at Naqada, Gerzean. (UC.4302, UC.4336, UC.4239.)
27. Two ivory harpoons from graves and two bone harpoons from the South Town settlement at Naqada. (UC.5208, UC.5210, UC.5290, UC.5289.)

ancient name of Naqada was *Nubt,* which means gold. It was used effectively in Gerzean and Protodynastic times to make jewellery and as gold foil to decorate stone, flint and wooden objects, and most of it was also no doubt swiftly stolen from the rich graves soon after interment. Lead may have been used to make small objects which have now disappeared because it is certainly found unworked in Gerzean graves as galena ore; this was the basic ingredient of the black kohl eye make-up. By determining the lead isotope ratio of pieces of galena from a grave at Naqada it has been established that the source of this ore was in the eastern desert about 180 km (110 miles) along the Wadi Hammamat in the Red Sea hills. Iron working was not known in Egypt until the New Kingdom, and the discovery of iron beads with dated gold types in graves at Gerzeh by Gerald Wainwright early in the twentieth century seemed sensational until it became evident that they were a unique find of hammered meteoric iron and therefore had not been smelted. This clarification does not, however, detract from the achievements of the Gerzean craftsmen in the mastery and expansion of diverse techniques, metal working not least among them, which formed part of the firm economic foundation which preceded the nation state.

5
Religion and art

Since the discovery of Predynastic cultures at the end of the nineteenth century interpretations of the religious beliefs and practices of the period have been numerous and speculative. Inference has to be based on the funerary customs, depictions found on the objects and some of the objects themselves, such as figurines. In the absence of a developed writing system these chance finds are open to different interpretations, often influenced by the fashions of modern times or the sex of the scholar! For instance, one or two past lady scholars championed the existence of the great 'mother' goddess to whom all other male gods were subordinate. Male scholarly predilections were for the interpretation of the motifs solely from the historic point of view, which involved extrapolating the known symbolism from Dynastic times back into the Predynastic. Now social anthropological models have entered the argument with emphasis on the dependence on agriculture and the development of a stratified society. One of the most attractive ideas to re-emerge recently is that the motifs on the decorated pottery and the potmarks are closely related to the development of the hieroglyphic script which existed from the Early Dynastic period, and that they convey messages. What is still not agreed upon is precisely what these messages say and a dictionary could be compiled from the various suggestions made since 1896.

The true picture of religious belief in the Predynastic may include quite a few of the suggestions which have been made, but there are one or two basic certainties. It is known from later religious and funerary practices that the Egyptians believed in an afterlife and made provision for it in their burials. The practice of elaborate burial of the dead with grave goods indicates that this belief goes back to the Predynastic and continued to develop. It is also known that the Egyptians took various precautions to safeguard the souls of their deceased through prophylactic amulets, spells and rituals, a custom also known in other ancient and modern societies. Amulets certainly existed in the Predynastic, and there are rare depictions of ceremonies. In later times there was a large pantheon of gods and goddesses, many of which were linked to, or personified by, animals. From the earliest times the Egyptians observed a predetermined pattern in the natural world which implied superhuman powers and a basic

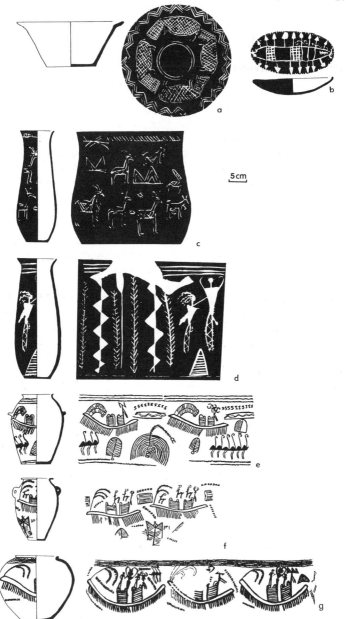

28. Examples of Amratian and Gerzean painted pottery motifs: (a-d) C class; (e-g) D class. (After Petrie and Needler.)

order which gave their religion a long tradition of conservatism. The depictions of various animals in the Predynastic can therefore sometimes be interpreted as representations of deities as well as prophylactic devices to ward off evil or ensure good hunting. Some figures were no doubt connected with ensuring fecundity, given a probable high infant mortality rate and the need to encourage the continued gift of the Nile's fertility. Pharaoh was also a god to his people and the development of a graded society with one ruler is echoed by the evolution of artistic subjects into the Protodynastic and Early Dynastic periods when the Upper Egyptian king, or his manifestation the bull, was often shown in a position of prominence undertaking important ceremonial duties.

Burial practices

The fact that it was most usual, but by no means consistent, to place the body in the grave with the head pointing towards the south and the face to the west has led to the notion that the Egyptians had already identified the locality of the 'land of the dead'. The foetal position for eternal rest is standard (figures 4 and 46) and quite often there might be more than one occupant in a grave, perhaps a man and a woman, two individuals of the same sex, an adult and a child, or a group of children. Their rest was sometimes disturbed by what may have been ritual dismemberment before interment. Many of the reported cases of dismemberment were probably caused by the actions of robbers or scavengers, but there remain some instances where the practice may have taken place. This might indicate some form of ancestor worship, particularly in cases when the head was removed and either deliberately placed somewhere else in the grave or replaced with something else. It may also simply be that relatives replaced a revered head when a robber had torn it off to get at a necklace, which seems to be the explanation for some later instances of dismemberment. The emplacement of grave goods was logical: small pots, cosmetic containers, amulets and palettes near the head and larger pots at either end of the grave. Some of the large storage jars in Gerzean graves were found to contain ashes with a thick vegetable paste on the top, as if some funerary feast and pouring of libation had taken place at the graveside before burial. The wavy-handled pottery jars often contain what was originally aromatic fat, the precursor to the seven sacred oils of the Old Kingdom, but sometimes have only good Nile mud as a substitute.

Depictions

The design elements on white cross-lined (C class) Naqada I pottery are restricted to geometric devices, hills, plants, domestic and desert animals (figure 28b), hippopotami (figure 28a) and crocodiles. More rarely there are depictions of humans (figure 28c) and boats (figure 28d). The hippopotamus was certainly respected and perhaps even worshipped. Apart from the paintings of them around the interior of bowls (figure 28a), amulets of pottery, bone and ivory in this form were also popular in the Amratian. The front cover of this book shows a pottery bowl from a woman's grave, the richest in the cemetery at El Mahasna, with modelled hippopotami around the rim. This grave also contained a male figurine with a penis sheath (figure 35g), and an ivory figure which has been identified as the first depiction of the mysterious animal of the god Seth, who, as god of chaotic forces, was connected with the hippopotamus in later times. From the prolific use of hippopotamus ivory in Predynastic and Dynastic times, it is certain that the animal was hunted and perhaps these charming early depictions (see also figure 32) served as protective devices against the marauding habits of the animal on the river banks. Occasionally human figures appear on C class pots. The man and woman on figure 28d are said to be dancing; they have also been identified as the great goddess and her male consort. There was certainly a cow-goddess, known from a relief of a cow's head with five stars on the horns on a slate palette from a grave at Gerzeh and from various potmarks (figure 30i), who is more likely to be Bat, the cow-goddess of Upper Egypt, than Hathor. The interior of a dish (figure 28b, UC.15319) has been identified as the top view of a boat with the oars on each side, but this unique piece is unprovenanced so its authenticity is dubious.

The repertoire of depictions on Gerzean pottery is greater and subsequently open to more interpretations. Certain elements seem to be standard, in various combinations such as boats with cabins, standards and banners, the Naqada plant, sycamore trees, shields, ostrich, gazelle, water lines, SSS signs, spirals and hills (figure 28e, f, g). It must be stated that some authors do not accept the identification of the boats, preferring them to represent watered land with a chief's residence, or a temple platform on stilts. The Naqada plant, which seems to sprout from a small pot, has been identified as an aloe, a sycamore tree, a rush with shoots and a relative of the date palm. The smaller divided tree is usually accepted as a sycamore, which was a sacred tree in historical depictions, from which the goddess Hathor poured

29. A marl ware pot of a Naqada II/III shape but with the type of painted decoration usually found on flat based jars with wavy handles. This may signify that the pot is genuine and the painting a forgery, although pots prepared for the antiquities market are not usually broken and repaired like this. (Courtesy of the School of Archaeology and Oriental Studies, University of Liverpool, E3035.)

libations. The identification of the long-necked birds which usually appear in rows has varied between ostrich and flamingo and back again. Although nobody disputes that the wavy lines at the top and bottom of the scenes denote water, the scattered SSS signs have been called numbers, libation water, or notations of weight. The spirals which sometimes appear on pots alone have been interpreted as nummulitic limestone, bread, a sign meaning 'surround everything' and as a simple decorative motif. Fortunately the blocked triangles which are usually linked together are universally identified as depictions of hills. These decorated pots are rare in settlement sites and not as frequent in graves as other

30. A selection of potmarks from Naqada including depictions of an elephant (a), a hippopotamus (b), an ibex (c), a boat (f), a crocodile (d), the cow-goddess (i), a bull horn standard (h), plants (e and g) and more enigmatic scratches (j-t) representing the contents, or the owner's mark. (After Petrie.)

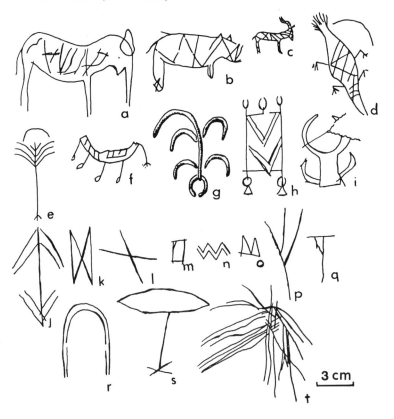

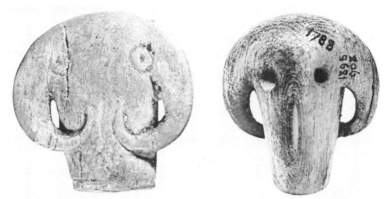

31. Bull's head amulets from Grave 1788 at Naqada, Naqada I/II: (left) hippopotamus ivory (UC.6005), and (right) elephant ivory (Ash.1895.908, courtesy of the Visitors of the Ashmolean Museum, Oxford).

types of pottery and it is probable that they were meant to confer special benefits on the dead. Perhaps the often repeated motifs were meant simply to ensure a continuation of spiritual life in an abundant Nilotic environment, or, in a more sophisticated way, they may be spells recording life, death and guaranteed resurrection. On some of these pots (figure 28g) there are schematic human figures. The goddess with raised arms is usually the central figure with smaller male attendants. Occasionally an ithyphallic male figure is depicted wearing a double plumed headdress, which was later the iconography of the fertility god Min of Koptos. Many of the design elements on the decorated pottery are repeated in incised drawings on the rocks of the wadis adjacent to the Nile valley from Upper Egypt to Nubia.

The standards on poles which appear on the boats are generally accepted as divine emblems and perhaps also the ensigns of clans or nomes. There is some agreement here because some of the standards are virtually identical with those of historic times such as the crossed arrows of the goddess Neith ⚔ and the emblem of the god Min ⚑, while others are identifiable signs. There is also an early tradition of marks incised into pottery, some of which represent animals, plants, boats and inferred signs (figure 30a-i) similar to those on the painted pots, and others which may be the owner's marks or descriptions of the contents or locality (figure 30j-t). These graffiti are found on sherds from settlements as well as on pots in graves and can justifiably be seen as a stage in the development of writing in which individual signs already had

32. Hippopotamus ivory carving of a hippopotamus with an inlaid stone eye from Grave 3823 at Badari, Naqada I. (UC.9573.)

33. (Below) Bone carving of a falcon from the South Town settlement at Naqada, probably late Naqada II. (UC.5288.)

34. A limestone lion said to be from the plundered cemetery at Gebelein, purchased by Petrie not far away at Thebes. The gash mouth and the tail curving up on the centre of the back signify that it is an early type, probably late Gerzean. (UC.15193.)

symbolic meanings, later to be followed by the phonetic values of the hieroglyphic script. Although there may have been some impetus provided from contact with Mesopotamia (figure 39), there is, therefore, evidence that the evolution of this script was indigenous.

Figures

Figures in the round of animals include the theriomorphic vessels in pottery or stone. Of these, birds (figure 12) and fish (figure 8) were the most popular, although frogs (figure 19) and other animals are also known. The fashion for these animal-shaped vessels, chiefly featuring hippopotami, began in the Badarian and continued into the Amratian. The painted birds and fish were popular in the Gerzean and it seems that, like the decorated pottery, they were meant to confer an afterlife which would include an abundance of Nile fauna. Apart from the birds that may be falcons (figure 33), they do not seem to represent divinities. The pottery model boats (figure 11), which copied papyrus river skiffs, can be included in the same genre and the symbolism conveyed by the boat in historic times was the journey through the underworld. Models of animals in pottery were mostly rougher models of bulls, cows, sheep and pigs, whilst in the rarer, fine flint sculptures birds, cows, snakes, bulls, sheep and hippopotami (figure 22) were depicted and such models of domestic animals can be assumed to be appeals to ancestors or divinities for an increase in the herd, or to be a record of such an event. The bull's head, or bucranium, which probably represents power and stability, was stylised into an amulet which looks like a mushroom slice (figure 31) in Naqada II and III. Another animal which conveyed a sense of guardianship and strength was the lion, and a particular way of depicting this animal in the round evolved from the late Predynastic. Lion models began to feature as game pieces in sets with dogs or hares, balls, brick shapes and rods and this style of game continued into the Early Dynastic period. At first the lion was carved with a gash mouth and its tail straight down between its haunches and then it began to grin and its tail curved up over its back in a question-mark shape during the Protodynastic (figure 34). This archaic style of lion sculpture persisted into the middle of the First Dynasty, when it was succeeded by the classic type of lion which had a closed mouth and its tail curved around its haunch, and the lioness was even depicted in a jewelled collar as if tame animals were used in the hunt.

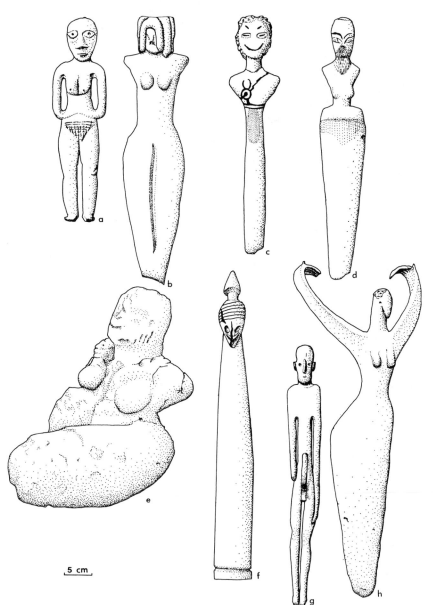

35. Human figurines: (a) ivory, from Badari, Badarian; (b) pottery, from Abadiyeh, Amratian/Gerzean; (c) vegetable paste on reed from El Amrah, Amratian/Gerzean; (d) pottery from Mostagedda, ?Badarian; (e) painted pottery from Ballas, Amratian; (f) ivory from Badari, Gerzean; (g) ivory from Mahasna, Amratian; (h) painted pottery from Ma'mariya, Amratian. (After P. J. Ucko, *Anthropomorphic Figurines of Predynastic Egypt,* 1968.)

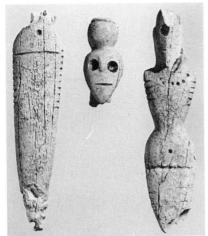 

36. (Left) Hippopotamus ivory figurine fragments from Grave 271 at Naqada, Gerzean. (UC.5252, UC.4253, UC.4251.)
37. (Right) Hippopotamus ivory pendant figurines from graves at Naqada, Gerzean. (UC.5455, UC.4290.)

The anthropomorphic figurines found in some graves from the Badarian period and, more rarely, in settlement sites, cannot be entirely explained as devices for sympathetic magic because, if those surviving are representative, it would signify a greater longing for females than for males. Of these female figures the Amratian pottery type with raised arms and a pinched, birdlike head (figure 35h) is like the dominating figures on the D class pottery and it has been suggested that they may be symbols of resurrection. The whole hippopotamus tusk with a bearded head at the tip (figure 35f) may be connected with the pairs of decorated tusks, usually one hollow and one solid, found in some Naqada I and II graves (figure 42k, l, m). These probably had a magical function, perhaps representing male and female elements. Two such tusks were found in the same Naqada I grave as the thin male figure (figure 35g) who wears a penis sheath. Many similar male figures in hippopotamus and elephant ivory were found in the great deposit of Protodynastic and Archaic objects in the temple at Hierakonpolis, thereby corroborating the idea that they had a votive function. The possibility that the other female figures, from the gross (figure 35e) to the sylph-like (figure 38), were concubine substitutes in the graves, is not borne out by their

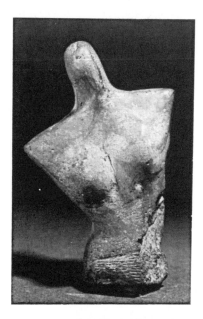
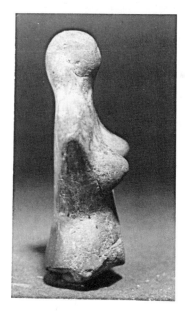

38. Pottery female torso with a tattoo on the back from the surface of a cemetery at Qau el Kebir. Thermoluminescence date 5020-2835 BC. (UC.9602.)

39. Two Mesopotamian cylinder seals found in Gerzean contexts in Egypt. At the top an ivory cylinder from Grave U364 at Hu and below a limestone cylinder from Grave 1863 at Naqada. (UC.10799 and UC.5374.)

association with the bodies of women and children. Some of the figurines, often crudely made, that were buried with children and adults could have been toys and in that case there would be no need for sexual correlations. In a few cases they could also be identified as servant figures (for example figure 36, head carrying a vessel) and it was a practice to include model estates in tombs from the Early Dynastic period. Unfortunately there is no connection between the number of figurines and the richness of the graves, which would be expected if they were meant to represent servants who would tend an estate in the afterlife. The 'best' figures made in the finer materials such as ivory are often the most schematic (figure 37) and some of those which lack sexual features (figure 36) are identified as female only by their hip/waist ratios. All the figurines are of an easily portable size and most have convenient narrow sections that could be gripped or suspended by thongs from the waist or neck like amulets. They did not occupy a special place in the tomb and are often found in containers or lying in piles of pottery. Whilst it is certain that none of these small human figures represents an early Egyptian mother goddess, various plausible explanations of their symbolism and the possibility of intriguing and varied usage for them still remain.

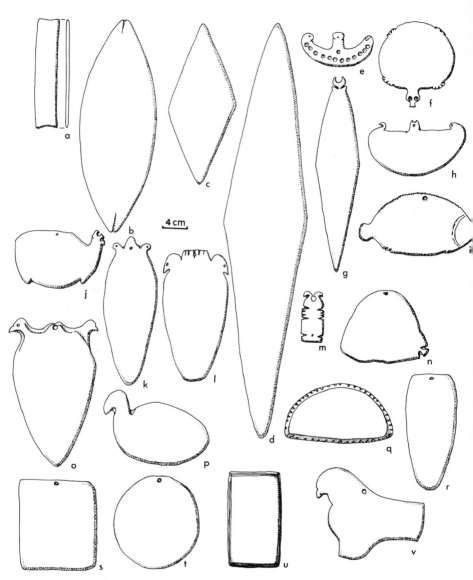

40. Slate cosmetic palettes: (a, b) Badarian; (c, d, f) Naqada I; (g, i, j, k, m) Naqada I-II; (e, h, l, n, p) Naqada II; (o, q, r, s, t, u, v) Naqada III. (After Petrie.)

6
Bodily adornment and organic remains

Bodily adornment

The Egyptian predilection for the elaborate eye make-up so garishly portrayed in modern films had an early beginning. The copper ore, malachite, and the lead ore, galena, were ground on cosmetic palettes to adorn the eyes and they probably also had a medicinal effect in helping to ward off flies. The so-called green slate palettes that were used for this purpose and deposited in graves, together with the pebbles used as grinding stones, are in most cases made of greywacke. They exhibit changes in fashion and their forms were linked with the magic and superstition of the other decorative arts of the period. In the Badarian (figure 40a, b) the forms were simple with grooves at each end so that the palettes could be carried on the person. During Naqada I the rhombic forms, like the similarly shaped flint knives, were popular (figure 40c, d), and palettes with the outlines of animals began to appear (figure 40f, j, k, m, i). Early in Naqada II a bulbous shape reminiscent of a boat with a cabin and decorated stern and prow was made (figure 40h). The palettes with double bird heads (figure 40l) and those depicting the Nile *bulti* fish, *Tilapia nilotica* (figure 40i, n), continued into Naqada II, becoming more stylised until the final approximations of Naqada III (figure 40o, q). By the Protodynastic the everyday palette had once again become simple (figure 40r, s, t, u), the rectangular palette with incised line border being the most popular (figure 40u). These rectangular palettes continued to be in vogue until the middle of the First Dynasty and occasionally the falcon, by this time linked with the god Horus, was sketched in palette form (figure 40v). During the period of unification the much larger decorative palettes, inspired by these common cosmetic palettes, were produced with commemorative scenes celebrating important events and dedicated in early temples.

Male and female heads were adorned with decorative combs and pins (figure 41) and forehead pendants (figure 42j) from Naqada I. The combs and pins often had animal and human heads (figure 42a-i) and of these the bird-headed hairpin remained popular throughout the Predynastic, but the ornate combs reduced to a simpler form (figure 42c). The tusks (figure

Predynastic Egypt

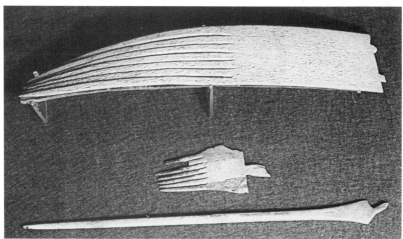

41. An ivory comb (76.09.5), a bone comb (76.09.5) and an ivory pin (76.09.2) from Tomb H45 at El Mahasna, Amratian. (Courtesy of Bolton Museums and Art Gallery and Bolton Metropolitan Borough Council.)

42k, l, m), which have been mentioned in connection with figurines, and the Naqada I and II incised tags of bone or stone which imitated them (figure 42n, o, p, q) were also perforated or grooved for suspension. Elise Baumgartel suggested that they were magical symbols for male and female, whilst more prosaically Flinders Petrie thought they were the stoppers from leather water bottles. They may have been containers as they have occasionally been found with lids. Ivory spoons which were probably used with cosmetics were known in the Badarian and by the later Predynastic they had the delicate form (figure 43) which persisted into the Early Dynastic period. Small vases of ivory and horn were probably also containers for cosmetics or resin.

The amulets which were worn for protection were accompanied by strings of beads which were made in a diversity of materials. A whole range of the available stones from desert regions near the Nile such as carnelian, diorite, garnet, haematite, steatite, serpentine, quartz, agate, limestone and calcite were employed. They were first chipped to shape and pierced with flint drills, then smoothed on a grinding stone with abrasive powder; no doubt copper drills were utilised for the bi-conical perforations of the later Predynastic. It is assumed that lapis lazuli was imported from Afghanistan through trade with Mesopotamia or Susiana, although there is a possibility that it was acquired near the oasis region to the west of the Nile valley.

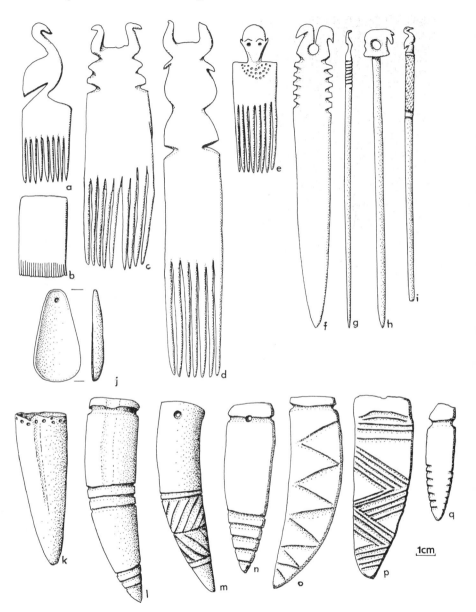

42. Bone and ivory combs (a-e), hairpins (f-i), forehead pendant (j), tusks (k-m), and tags (n-q), Naqada I-II. (After Petrie.)

43. Bone spoon with a figure of a falcon on the handle, from Grave 244 at Ballas, Naqada III. (UC.5479.)

44. (Below) A selection of beads and amulets: (a) ring beads; (b) cylinder beads; (c) barrel beads; (d) spheroids; (e) pendants; (f) bull head amulet; (g) cow head amulet; (h, i) flies; (j-n) shell pendants and fancy beads; Naqada I-III. (After Brunton.)

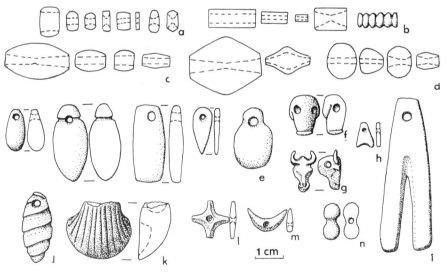

Obsidian may have come from Ethiopia and green amazon stone
(microcline feldspar) from Tibesti in the Sahara. Shells made into
beads or bracelets came from the Red Sea, the Nile and the
Mediterranean. The large freshwater *Spatha* shells and the
smaller mussels *(Unio)* were often kept intact and used as
cosmetic palettes. Tubulets of pink coral from the Red Sea were
made into cylinder beads. On quartz and steatite beads the glaze
containing malachite produced the greenish-blue colour which
imitated the rarer turquoise. These glazed stone beads were
common in Badarian graves and in one a large belt of them was
found around a man's waist. Later they were replaced by
moulded green/blue faience (glazed composition). This quartz-
based, fired material remained very popular throughout Egyptian
history and it was also produced in red and yellow. Clay was
moulded into beads and painted red and black in the late
Predynastic. Copper was used for rings, bracelets and beads and
some beads of gold and silver have survived. The most common
shapes of beads were rings (figure 44a), cylinders (figure 44b),
barrels (figure 44c) and spheroids (figure 44d), but simple and
ornate pendants were produced (figure 44e, j, k, m, n). Amulets
such as bulls' and cows' heads (figure 44f, g) and flies (figure 44h,
i) were interspersed in the strings. Because of their frequency, the
typology of beads and amulets can be a useful corollary in the
relative dating of grave groups.

Organic remains
    The generally good preservation afforded by the desert graves
has resulted in the endurance of many pieces of organic material,
including plants. The ivory and bone accessories described above
are included in this category, but there are also remains of leather
and textiles associated with the bodies. Leather was made from
calf, gazelle, goat and sheep skin, and it was frequently used to
make a pouch and tube to contain the male testicles and penis.
This penis sheath was attached by two thongs from the top and
bottom to a waist band (figure 35). Aprons and cloaks were made
in leather, which was sometimes decorated with geometric
paintings in white, yellow, black or blue, and leather sandals with
thongs were worn. There were also cushions of leather stuffed
with vegetable matter and cosmetics were carried in leather bags
which were placed near the hands of the deceased. Flax was
woven into fine and coarse linen, fragments of which have been
found in the graves, and a famous white cross-lined bowl from a
grave at Badari depicts people working at a loom (UC.9547). It

seems that linen was occasionally used as a canvas. Fragments of linen from Gebelein, now in the Turin museum, have a painted scene in red and black of men rowing and steering large boats. Apart from the jewellery and clothing worn by individuals, the evidence from figurines (figure 38) signifies that some people may have applied decoration directly to their bodies in the form of cicatrices or tattoos.

The human bodies themselves are often well preserved, due to the desiccating effect of the desert sand in which they were buried, with at least some of the soft tissue and hair remaining (figure 46). This has made various observations possible, such as the confirmation that circumcision was an early practice in Egypt and that some people suffered from chronic constipation. It has also established that artificial mummification involving the removal of the brain and the viscera did not take place in prehistory. Further palaeopathological examinations have been made by the use of X-rays which reveal such conditions as arthritis. If no soft tissue survives, the skeletons alone can be sexed, aged and analysed for racial characteristics and pathology, thus making demographic studies feasible. This sort of approach is now more common, whereas in the past it was variable and the bodies were often ignored and re-buried whilst the objects from the graves were retained for museum collections.

On a properly conducted settlement excavation the collection of animal bone is systematic. Sieving can recover the smaller bones of rodents, birds and fish and the resulting finds are sorted by the zoologist to separate identifiable bones and teeth from scraps. The morphological attribute data is then coded for computer analysis, making possible the generation of multiple

45. Bone amulet of an ibex head which was found tied around the ankle of the male body in Grave 5409 at Badari, Badarian. (UC.9123.)

46. Grave N7067 at Naga ed-Dêr, which contained the well preserved contracted body of an adult female with a goatskin garment on her back and other traces of coarse linen clothing. (Courtesy of the Museum of Fine Arts, Boston.)

cross-clarification tables and useful statistics of the percentage of domestic species in archaeological sites, as well as their age at death. This gives insight into the herding and butchering practices and suggests that in settlements near to the valley mature cattle, goats, sheep and pigs were utilised for protein, whilst flocks of young goats and sheep were herded seasonally in the wadis. The presence of dogs can be ascertained from a large number of gnawed animal bones, reduced numbers of long-bone shafts, ribs, scapulae and vertebrae and a greater percentage of inedible parts, without the remains of the canines themselves. The Nile was fished for perch *(Lates niloticus), bulti (Tilapia),* puffer fish *(Tetrodon)* and catfish *(Bagrus, Synodontis* and *Claridae).* Turtles, crocodiles, hippopotami and gazelles were hunted. One find at Hierakonpolis suggests that asses were used as draft animals in the south as well as the north, where they are known from Maadi.

Archaeo-botanical examination of the plant remains in graves and settlements is now an established procedure. Smaller plant remains are collected by the flotation method from soil samples. The graves were often roofed or lined with boughs of sycamore

(Ficus sycomorus) or *Tamarix* and the corpses were enclosed in lashed wood and twig frameworks on wooden biers of *Acacia,* or in wooden boxes in later graves. The bodies were covered with mats made of reed *(Cyperus alopecroides)* or halfa grass *(Desmostachya bipinnata),* bound together with intertwined or cross threads with the ends turned over at the edges. Baskets were made of straps of dom palm *(Hyphaene thebaica)* and date palm *(Phoenix dactylifera).* Wheat *(Triticum)* and barley *(Hordeum)* and various herbs, weeds and reeds from occupation sites signify that a wetter climate in the wadis prevailed in the early and middle Predynastic, making them favourable for agriculture and pasture. The consumption of such vegetation for artefacts, grazing and fuel combined with climatic change may have encouraged the general move closer to the Nile valley in the late Predynastic.

Analyses of wood, seeds and resins can also indicate the ancient trade routes. Pine, cypress and juniper are not native trees in Egypt and were probably imported from Palestine; cedar certainly came from south Syria. Pieces of resin are often found in Predynastic graves associated with small pieces of malachite and galena and it may have been used as a medicament. True resin is extracted from pine and fir trees and it could have come from Byblos by the sea route along the Mediterranean coast.

Organic remains can also provide samples for the chronometric dating method which consists of measuring the decay of the carbon-14 isotope, based on a half-life of 5568 years. This was first used by the American Willard Libby in the 1950s to obtain absolute ages from excavated material. Unfortunately the materials used to obtain Predynastic dates were taken from contaminated museum objects and therefore produced the inaccurate date range of 4623-4495 BC for Naqada I and 3845-3494 BC for Naqada II. Whilst the radiocarbon dates for Egyptian material back to 2000 BC agree with the historical dates, the historical chronologies calculated for the third and fourth millennia BC from a Middle Kingdom astronomical event and various king lists are themselves disputed, and the carbon-14 dates for this period were met with scepticism by Egyptologists because they were consistently too late.

Since those early days, radiocarbon dating has been much refined and methods are now more sensitive and accurate. A fundamental necessity is well contexted, uncontaminated samples, from the same event, preferably collected as such in the field. The material used for testing is most often wood, or charcoal, but results have been obtained from hair, skin and shell. Grain and seed samples can be tested as it is now possible to date very small amounts (5 mg) using accelerated mass spectrometry, which also makes the sampling of valuable museum objects more feasible. The radiocarbon dates produced are converted from years bp (before present) to years BC (before Christ), so that they can be compared with dates derived from other sources. They are corrected with tables giving tree-ring calibrations (from the dendrochronologically dated growth rings of the long-lived bristle cone pine) and the dates are usually given as a midpoint and a standard deviation in years BC, for example 4295 ± 175, which signifies a range of several hundred years rather than a point in time. It is possible to arrive at greater precision by combining dates and statistically averaging them to reduce the rate of error, if there are enough acceptable results from one context. The new pioneer in this field is Fekri Hassan. His collection of corrected and averaged carbon-14 dates for the Predynastic of Upper and Lower Egypt accords fairly well with the framework chronology extrapolated from the historical dates. It also confirms the sequence set up for the cultures of Upper Egypt in the early days of research. The following is a chronological chart of the tree-ring calibrated radiocarbon dates for Upper and Lower Egypt giving the statistical age range from available determinations. The left-hand column is years BC.

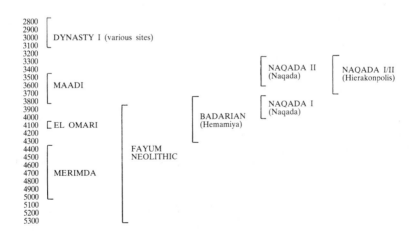

7
Foreign contacts and modern trends

Petrie was unwittingly the discoverer of the Predynastic cultures of Upper Egypt and the foundations of ancient Egyptian civilisation when he excavated the cemetery at Naqada in 1895. So different were the bodies and the artefacts he unearthed from those he knew from over ten years' excavation in Egypt that he announced the discovery as the entry of a 'New Race' into Egypt during the politically disrupted First Intermediate period (2181-2040 BC) after the Old Kingdom. Jacques de Morgan, a far less competent French archaeologist, who found Predynastic and Protodynastic graves at Abydos and Naqada in 1896, had recognised them straightaway as prehistoric. When Petrie saw these finds in Cairo on his following year's expedition to Egypt he became aware that his own discoveries were early, but it was too late to correct the *Naqada and Ballas* report which had already gone to press. Instead, his legacy became the painstaking scientific method which he applied to the analysis of excavated Predynastic material, culminating in the publication of his Sequence Dating in the *Diospolis Parva* report of 1901. The method he invented, now called seriation by statisticians, led to him being called one of the greatest applied mathematicians of the nineteenth century.

Many other researchers have been involved with Predynastic studies since then. One of the most indefatigable was Elise Baumgartel, who devoted her life to recovering and re-interpreting the scattered objects from Petrie's incompletely published Naqada excavations (he was not always a paragon). Many of her resulting theories were somewhat striking and have been disputed, particularly her emphasis on the contacts with western Asia and even an invasion to account for the stylistic changes of Naqada II. Other scholars also emphasised the role outside influence played in the unification of Egypt and post-ulated the influx of the 'Dynastic Race'. The most factually based work on foreign objects and foreign stylistic influences in Predynastic contexts in Egypt (figure 39) was that of Helene Kantor, who meticulously listed those found up to the 1950s to-gether with their Palestinian, Syrian and Mesopotamian counter-parts. The resemblances established with south-west Asia for the Badarian and Naqada I are the most tenuous, but there is no doubt that there was a trading network with the exchange of ideas

and goods which increased throughout the Predynastic. Protodynastic trading encampments were found between El Arish and
El Beda on the north-east road to Palestine by the Israeli
archaeologist Eliezer Oren in 1972. These surface finds consisted
of stone tools, stone containers, flint and metal objects of
Egyptian type and Egyptian and Canaanite broken pottery
vessels in the ratio of 5:1. The work of Kaiser and others such as
Anthony Arkell and Peter Ucko has shown that the change from
Naqada I to II was more continuous than had been previously
supposed and some infiltration from the eastern desert could
easily account for the innovations of Naqada II. During the
Naqada III expansionist phase exploitation of the natural
resources of the south such as gold, copper and game animals
probably took place and the presence of distinctive Nubian
pottery, frequently with incised decoration (N class), in Upper
Egyptian cemeteries has been attested, as has Egyptian pottery in
Lower Nubia.

Kantor also demolished Petrie's concept of the Semainean
culture at the end of the Predynastic, which in Petrie's view
marked a break caused by invasion, preferring to see it as the
later part of the Gerzean from which the First Dynasty more
immediately arose. Whilst fuller discussion of the process of
unification and the rise of the early dynasties with proper
consideration of the commemorative artefacts must await treatment in another volume, it should be stated here that the Naqada
III phase now recognised by most scholars represents a period of
social change and increased contact with Lower Egypt and from
there with western Asia, but no break in continuity with Naqada
II. This is dramatically confirmed by new work in the Delta and
re-analysis of the material from Maadi, where links with the
Levant are strongest, as well as by the Palestinian pottery being
found in the context of a possible Gerzean religious complex and
the Protodynastic élite tombs at Hierakonpolis. The cultural
continuity now evident means that there is no need to postulate
an invasion of foreigners to account for the rise of the dynasties.
The broad-skulled 'Dynastic Race' of the Early Dynastic and Old
Kingdom could easily be men of the Delta who were blended into
the nation state. Archaeology is revealing the solidly based
economic development that was causative in the thrust from
Hierakonpolis. The magnitude of production and population as
well as the developed hierarchies is now being aligned with the
evidence from pictorial representations to account for the
changes that were taking place.

It is no longer necessary to identify a foreign pottery or wood import on stylistic grounds alone. The clay and plant sources can be analysed to prove or disprove the argument. Sweeping statements that there was no difference in mortuary and domestic wares are disproved by the dogged statistical analysis of thousands of potsherds which reveals a greater abundance of rough wares in the settlements and special functional pottery types which were not found in graves. Comprehensive study and analysis of the products of flint knapping is producing factual evidence for testing hypotheses about production centres. The identification and quantification of mammal, reptile and fish bones gives a clearer picture of animal domestication and hunting techniques. The new and corrected information also makes feasible the re-evaluation of old material and excavators' unpublished manuscripts can be used to delve for evidence that was not thought important at the beginning of the twentieth century. Museum collections can be 're-excavated' by the careful conservation and reconstruction of previously untreated material to produce objects that are new to science. Within the limits imposed by the records this makes possible the fuller publication of inadequately covered material from the past, which can then be analysed and fitted into the broader picture to stimulate further thought and discussion. In the expanding field of Quaternary studies in Egypt, geomorphological and sedimentary investigations make the regional study of Pleistocene and Holocene Nilotic shifts and floods and their effects on human habitation less speculative. Several expeditions are elucidating the earlier prehistory of the Nile valley at palaeolithic and neolithic sites in Egypt and Nubia. Finally Egyptian archaeology is coming of age as it attracts and takes advantage of so many specialists. It is an exciting time for collaborative, multidisciplinary, prehistoric research with modern techniques and the potential for continued discovery. The essence of the statement of Harry Smith, one of the most penetrating and inspiring minds in modern Egyptology, that 'History is best served by sticking to the evidence', is now being realised in this field.

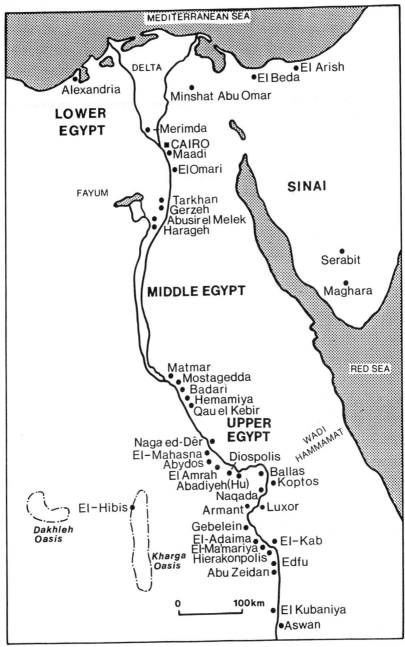

47. Map of Egypt showing Predynastic sites.

72

8
Further reading

There are few general books in print on Predynastic Egypt and therefore one or two of the classic older titles have been included here in the hope that the interested reader might be able to obtain reprints or library copies.

Adams, Barbara. *The Fort Cemetery at Hierakonpolis (Excavated by John Garstang).* Kegan Paul International, 1988.

Arkell, Anthony J. *The Prehistory of the Nile Valley.* Handbuch der Orientalistik, 1. Band, 2. Abschnitt A, Lieferung 1. Brill, 1975.

Arkell, A. J., and Ucko, Peter J. 'Review of Predynastic Development in the Nile Valley', *Current Anthropology,* volume 6 (1965) 145-66.

Baumgartel, Elise J. *The Cultures of Prehistoric Egypt.* Oxford University Press, volume I 1955, volume II 1960.

Capart, Jean. *Primitive Art in Egypt.* London, 1905.

Fairservis, Walter A. *Hierakonpolis — The Graffiti and the Origins of Egyptian Hieroglyphic Writing.* Occasional Papers in Anthropology, number 2. Vassar College, New York, 1983.

Hoffman, Michael A. *Egypt before the Pharaohs.* Routledge Kegan Paul, 1979.

Hoffman, M. A., and others. *The Predynastic of Hierakonpolis.* Egyptian Studies Association Publication number 1, Cairo and Illinois, 1982.

Mond, Robert, and Myers, Oliver H. *Cemeteries of Armant 1* (2 volumes). Egypt Exploration Society, 1937.

Needler, Winifred. *Predynastic and Archaic Egypt in the Brooklyn Museum.* Wilbour Monographs (IX), Brooklyn, 1984.

Petrie, W. M. Flinders. *Diospolis Parva: The Cemeteries of Abadiyeh and Hu 1898-9.* Egypt Exploration Fund Memoirs 21 (1901), reprinted 1973.

Petrie, W. M. F. and Quibell, J. E. *Naqada and Ballas.* Egyptian Research Account, 1896, reprinted by Aris and Phillips, 1974.

Petrie, W. M. F. *Prehistoric Egypt* and *Corpus of Prehistoric Pottery and Palettes.* British School of Archaeology in Egypt, 1920 and 1921, reprinted in one volume by Aris and Phillips, 1974.

Ucko, P. J. *Anthropomorphic Figurines of Predynastic Egypt and Neolithic Crete with Comparative Material from the Prehistoric Near East and Mainland Greece.* Royal Anthropological Institute Occasional Papers 24, 1968.

9
Museums to visit

Museums with Predynastic objects in their Egyptology collections include:

United Kingdom

Ashmolean Museum of Art and Archaeology, Beaumont Street, Oxford OX1 2PH. Telephone: Oxford (0865) 278000.

Birmingham Museum and Art Gallery, Chamberlain Square, Birmingham B3 3DH. Telephone: 021-235 2834.

Bolton Museum and Art Gallery, Le Mans Crescent, Bolton, Lancashire BL1 1SE. Telephone: Bolton (0204) 22311, extension 2191.

British Museum, Great Russell Street, London WC1B 3DG. Telephone: 01-636 1555.

Castle Museum, Norwich, Norfolk NR1 3JU. Telephone: Norwich (0603) 611277, extension 275.

City of Bristol Museum and Art Gallery, Queens Road, Bristol BS8 1RL. Telephone: Bristol (0272) 299771.

Durham University Oriental Museum, Elvet Hill, Durham DH1 3TH. Telephone: Durham (0385) 66711.

Fitzwilliam Museum, Trumpington Street, Cambridge CB2 1RB. Telephone: Cambridge (0223) 332900.

Liverpool Museums, William Brown Street, Liverpool L3 8EN. Telephone: 051-207 0001 or 5451.

Maidstone Museum and Art Gallery, St Faith's Street, Maidstone, Kent ME14 1LH. Telephone: Maidstone (0622) 54497.

Manchester Museum, The University of Manchester, Oxford Road, Manchester M13 9PL. Telephone: 061-273 3333.

Museum of the School of Archaeology and Oriental Studies, University of Liverpool, PO Box 147, Liverpool L69 3BX. Telephone: 051-709 6022 extension 3086.

Petrie Museum of Egyptian Archaeology, University College London, Gower Street, London WC1E 6BT. Telephone: 01-387 7050 extension 2884.

Royal Museum of Scotland, Chambers Street, Edinburgh EH1 1JF. Telephone: 031-225 7534.

Sheffield City Museum, Weston Park, Sheffield, South Yorkshire S10 2TP. Telephone: Sheffield (0742) 768588.

Swansea Museum (University College of Swansea and Royal Institution of South Wales Museum), Victoria Road, Swansea,

West Glamorgan SA1 1SN. Telephone: Swansea (0792) 53763.
Towneley Hall Art Gallery and Museums, Burnley, Lancashire
BB11 3RQ. Telephone: Burnley (0282) 24213.

Australia
Ancient History Teaching Collection, Macquarie University,
Sydney, New South Wales 2109.
Nicholson Museum, University of Sydney, Sydney, New South
Wales 2006.

Egypt
Aswan Museum, Island of Elephantine, Aswan.
Egyptian Antiquities Museum, Tahrir Square, Cairo.
Luxor Museum, Luxor.

Europe
Ägyptisches Museum, Schlossstrasse 70, 1000 Berlin 19, West
  Germany.
Ägyptisches Museum, Staatliche Museen, Bodestrasse 1 - 3, 102
Berlin, East Germany.
Medelhavsmuseet, Järntorget 84, Stockholm, Sweden.
Musée du Louvre, Palais du Louvre, 75003 Paris, France.
Musées Royaux d'Art et d'Histoire, Avenue J. F. Kennedy, 1040
Brussels, Belgium.
Museo Egizio, Palazzo dell' Accademia delle Scienze, Via
Accademia delle Scienze 6, Turin, Italy.

United States of America
The Brooklyn Museum, 188 Eastern Parkway, Brooklyn, New
York 11238.
Cleveland Museum of Art, 11150 East Boulevard, Cleveland,
Ohio 44106.
Metropolitan Museum of Art, 5th Avenue at 82nd Street, New
York 10028.
Museum of Fine Arts, Huntingdon Avenue, Boston, Mas-
sachusetts 02115.
Robert H. Lowie Museum of Anthropology, 103 Kroeber Hall,
University of California, Berkeley, California 94720.
University of Chicago Oriental Institute Museum, 1155 East 58th
Street, Chicago, Illinois 60637.
University Museum, University of Pennsylvania, 33rd and Spruce
Streets, Philadelphia, Pennsylvania 19104.

Index